Rowing

Produced in collaboration with
the Amateur Rowing Association

Produced for A & C Black by

Monkey Puzzle Media Ltd
Gissings Farm, Fressingfield
Suffolk IP21 5SH

Published in 2007 by

A & C Black Publishers Ltd
38 Soho Square, London W1D 3HB
www.acblack.com

First edition 2007

Note: While every effort has been made to ensure
that the content of this book is as technically accurate
and as sound as possible, neither the author nor the
publisher can accept responsibility for any injury or
loss sustained as a result of the use of this material.

This book is produced using paper that is made from
wood grown in managed, sustainable forests. It is
natural, renewable and recyclable. The logging and
manufacturing processes conform to the
environmental regulations of the country of origin.

Acknowledgements
Cover and inside design by James Winrow and
Tom Morris for Monkey Puzzle Media Ltd.
Cover photograph courtesy of Getty Images
(John Gichigi).
We would like to thank the following for permission
to reproduce photos; Amateur Rowing Association
(ARA) pages 20 (left and right), 21 (all), 42 (top); AP/PA
Photos pages 60 (Tom Hevezi), 61 (Koji Sasahara);
Birmingham Schools page 16; Dave Godfrey page 15
(top); Dries Hettinga, Brunel University page 51;
Gerard Brown pages 7, 11 (top-right), 12, 13 (top and
bottom), 14 (bottom), 22, 32, 33, 34, 35 (left and
right), 39, 40, 41, 43 (top and bottom), 44, 46, 48, 53;
Graeme Nicholson page 10; Graham Tonks page 8
(left); London Youth Rowing (Penny Cuthbert) pages
5, 6, 17, 18, 23, 30, 52; Marty Aitken page 11 (top-,
middle- and bottom-left), 26, 27 (left and right), 28
(left and right), 29 (top- and bottom-left and right);
Maurice Coughlan page 31; PA Archive/PA Photos
pages 9 (top-left), 9 (bottom-left – Fiona Hanson), 36
(Chris Young), 37 (Chris Young); Paul Vernall page 49;
Peter Spurrier/Intersport Images pages 4, 9 (top-right
and bottom-right), 14 (top), 15 (bottom), 47, 50;
Salters Steamers, Oxford page 42 (bottom);
www.veniceworld.com (Paola de Calò) page 8 (right).
All illustrations by Dave Saunders.

Every effort has been made to trace copyright holders
and to obtain their permission for the use of copyright
material. The publisher apologises for any errors or
omissions in the above list and would be grateful if
notified of any corrections that should be incorporated
in future reprints or editions of this book.

Written by Jim Flood drawing on material provided by
the Amateur Rowing Association

KNOW THE GAME is a registered trademark.

Printed and bound in China by C&C Offset Printing
Co., Ltd.

Note: Throughout the book players and officials are
referred to as 'he'. This should, of course, be taken
to mean 'he or she' where appropriate.

CONTENTS

FOREWORD BY SIR STEVE REDGRAVE CBE

I am delighted to be involved with this new version of *Know the Game: Rowing*. Rowing is an increasingly popular sport and is growing at an unprecedented rate. UK crews are consistently successful at the Olympics and World Championships.

National Lottery funding has meant we have been able to help rowing clubs encourage the development of rowing in state schools. We are also widening participation further by adapting rowing equipment for people with disabilities. Our aim is to remove barriers to participation, real and perceived, so that rowing becomes truly a 'sport for all'.

Rowing indoors on rowing machines is now the fastest-growing part of our sport. Rowing machines provide a mass-participation sport in their own right, as well as being a gateway to rowing on water.

People are increasingly aware of the importance of sport in promoting health and wellbeing. Rowing provides demanding, low-impact exercise for the whole body. In addition, the teamwork developed through participation in sport is a vital lifelong skill. Rowing has much to contribute in this respect – to be successful, crews must learn to row with each other and for each other. The sense of feeling a boat respond as the crew works together in absolute harmony is exhilarating in every sense.

I hope that some of you who read this book will find yourselves competing in the 2012 Olympics.

I wish you every success in rowing.

Sir Steve Redgrave CBE

 A team of juniors enjoying practice.

INTRODUCTION

The aim of this book is to provide you with an overview of the sport of rowing. You might be someone who is interested in learning to row, you might be a rowing coach looking for support material in your teaching of rowing, or you might be in a position to open up opportunities for sport in your local community.

AIMS

Having read this book, you will be able to:

- identify the most common types of boats and equipment used in the sport

- understand the key differences between rowing, sculling and indoor rowing

- explain the importance of using the rowing technique that is most effective in moving boats quickly

- describe the main parts and phases of the rowing and sculling strokes

- understand the key aspects of safety procedures in rowing

- understand the importance of hydration, hygiene and nutrition when taking part in rowing

- explain the roles of different participants in the sport: i.e. rowers, coaches and coxes

- understand the wide opportunities that rowing offers in respect of health, fitness, teamwork and social interaction

- have a broad idea of the competition structure

- know where to go for further information.

Indoor rowing is now recognised as a sport in its own right.

St. Neots girls' team take a break
during practice.

ROWING'S EARLY DAYS

The first recorded history of rowing a boat with oars, instead of using paddles, appears on Greek pottery dated around 800 BC and shows a *pentekonter,* an ancient warship with a single row of 25 oars on each side.

THE TRIREME

By 500 BC, the Greek ships had developed into the trireme, a fearsome warship with 170 oarsmen that could outmanoeuvre sailing ships in order to ram them. It is highly likely that as part of the training of crews, races took place between triremes.

EARLY ROWING CONTESTS

The word 'regatta' comes from the Italian word *regata,* which described a series of rowing races. From around 1250 there were races in Venice, Italy to improve the skills of the city's oarsmen. These races still take place today, and now include oarswomen as well as oarsmen.

By 1700 rowing had become a popular sport in London, with competitions between boats rowed by apprentice watermen on the River Thames. The watermen were the taxi drivers of their day, ferrying people around the waterways of London. The winner of a race held in 1715 was awarded a coat and badge, and the race became known as the Doggett's Coat and Badge race. This is the longest continuously recorded sporting event in the world.

 A re-enactment of an early regatta.

THE BOAT RACE

The first race between Oxford and Cambridge universities – now known as 'the Boat Race' – took place in 1829, in boats that were very different from modern racing boats.

 Oxford beat Cambridge in the 1954 Boat Race.

HENLEY ROYAL REGATTA

Henley Royal Regatta was first held in 1839, and today is the equivalent of Wimbledon in tennis. Henley was the rowing venue for the 1908 and 1948 Olympics. Racing and winning at Henley is the ambition of every aspiring rower, and each year the event draws top international crews from all over the world.

The Trinity College, Dublin crew competes in the Henley Royal Regatta.

ROWING IN THE OLYMPICS

Rowing has been an Olympic sport since 1896, when the modern form of the games began in Athens. That first year, the weather was too bad to race – the first Olympic rowing actually took place in 1900. In recent years the Great Britain rowing team has achieved outstandingly good results at the Olympic Games and World Championships.

The British coxless four of Matthew Pinsent, Tim Foster, Steve Redgrave and James Cracknell winning – and celebrating – gold at the 2004 Olympics. Steve Redgrave set a new record by winning his fifth consecutive gold medal for rowing.

EQUIPMENT IN USE

Trying to understand the amount and range of equipment used in rowing can be quite overwhelming. This chapter aims to guide you through the main components, such as oars, boats and rowing machines, and explains how these are used.

OARS

The oars, often called the 'blades', are used by the rower to lever the boat through the water. Beginners often think that the ends of the oars move through the water but close observation shows this is not true.

If you watch a rowing boat carefully you will see that it moves forward past the 'puddles' made by the end of the oar. Effectively the end of the blade (the 'spoon') in the water does not move. It is a fixed point for the oar, which acts as a lever to move the boat forward, and is therefore the fulcrum (see diagram below).

In this picture the rower in the foreground is making a puddle with the oars. The rower in the background is leaving the puddles behind as the boat moves forward.

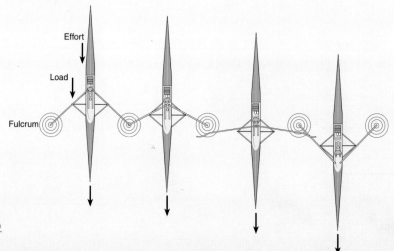

SLIDING SEATS

When you examine a racing-style rowing boat, you'll see that the seat is on wheels, allowing it to slide up and down. Also, the shoes you wear are fixed into the boat. Both these features allow the rower to take a much longer, more efficient stroke, and therefore to move the boat further (see photo right).

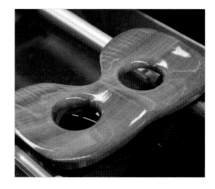

A sliding seat allows this range of movement.

Before sliding seats were developed, rowers put grease on the seat of their pants to be able to slide up and down as they rowed!

BLADE ACTION

When you watch rowers in action you will notice that the blades are turned flat so that they are parallel to the water. This reduces wind resistance. When the blades are in the water, this is known as the 'square' position. When the blades are flat, it is known as the 'feathered' position.

BOAT CONSTRUCTION

Until around thirty years ago boats were made of wood and many clubs have fine examples of them still in use. If you have an opportunity to look at one, examine the wonderful craft skills that went into making it.

Modern boats are made from varieties of glass-reinforced plastic and other composite materials such as Kevlar, carbon fibre and epoxy resin. Boats and oars are now the products of very sophisticated design and technological processes, which are used to create boats that are lighter, stronger and require less effort to move them through the water.

HULL CONSTRUCTION

The hulls of wooden boats used to be made from thin sheets of wood called veneers – a similar method to Native American canoe construction. Modern boats use the same construction techniques as racing cars – and are often made in the same factory.

 A modern, lightweight rowing boat, ready for the crew to climb in.

RIGGERS AND GATES

At one time the oar pivoted in a rowlock on the side of the boat. As boats became narrower the rowlock, now called a gate, began to be fixed on the end of the rigger. (The rigger is a triangular metal structure fitted to the side of the boat. The correct name for the rigger is an outrigger, but the name has become shortened with use.) The gate has a latch, which is unscrewed and lifted up, then the oar is fitted inside and the screw tightened to lock the oar in. This prevents the blade from lifting out.

BOAT CARE

- Boats are very fragile and more damage is done to boats in the boathouse than on the water.
- Care must be taken when carrying boats to avoid contact with sharp objects such as the corners of racks and the riggers of other boats.

If the gate latch is not screwed up firmly, the blade can come out of the rigger, causing the boat to capsize.

The rigger (triangular frame) and gate (which holds the oar in place) on a modern boat.

ROWING AND SCULLING

Rowing, or sweep-oar rowing as it is sometimes known, uses one oar per person. Sculling uses an oar in each hand.

TYPES OF SCULLING AND ROWING BOATS

The drawings below show the schematic layout of different racing boats. Try to identify them when you see them on the water.

All eights have a cox (short for coxswain – the person who steers the boat). Some fours and nearly all pairs, doubles and singles are coxless. In a competition programme you will see boats listed as: 1x, 2x, 2-, 4-, 4+, 4x, 4x+, 8+ and 8x+. Can you guess which categories of boat these are? You will also see either a W or M in front to denote a women's or men's event.

Can you tell which is rowing and which is sculling?

Racing boat layout.

The answers are:
Eight = 8+, Octuple = 8X+, Quadruple = 4X (4X+ with a cox), Four = 4- (4+ with a cox), Double = 2X, Pair = 2- (2+ with a cox), Single = 1X.

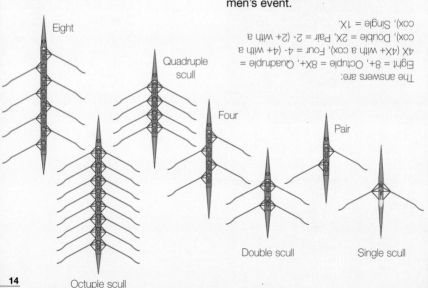

Eight

Quadruple scull

Four

Pair

Octuple scull

Double scull

Single scull

WHERE PEOPLE ROW

Most rowing takes place on rivers or lakes. Some rowing and racing takes place on the sea in boats that are specially designed to cope with waves and rough water.

ROWING IN THE SEA

Coastal and offshore rowing is growing in popularity. Originally this was done in traditional boats, like those used by pilots whose job it was to meet large boats and guide them into harbour. Although modern boats are based on these designs, they are usually now made from modern materials. Traditional wooden boats are still used in the sport of skiff racing, which takes place mainly on the River Thames.

Coastal rowing can be quite a rough ride.

ROWING AND YOUNG PEOPLE

Rowing can put more stress on a growing body than sculling. People under the age of 16 are encouraged to scull.

A fun rowing event – fancy dress is optional!

INDOOR ROWING

The development of rowing machines (often referred to as ergometers or simply 'ergos') has resulted in a huge growth in the sport of indoor rowing – the fastest-growing mass-participation sport in the country. It is estimated that there are over 500,000 people regularly using rowing machines for general fitness and competition.

There are now local, regional, national and world championships for a wide range of age groups and categories.

Sophisticated electronics and computer technology on today's ergos provides you with a display showing how hard you are working, how much energy you have expended and your predicted time for a set distance.

The 1:51 showing in the display in the diagram below indicates a predicted time of 1 minute 51 seconds for a distance of 500m – that is if you are able to maintain the same rate and pressure of rowing. Races are usually over 1,000 or 2,000m, so the predicted time for 500m shows how close you are to achieving your target.

Indoor rowing contests are increasingly popular.

ERGOMETERS

- The name 'ergometer' is derived from two Greek words *ergon* and *metron*.
- *Ergon* means work and *metron* means measure.
- An ergometer displays your power output in watts.
- To measure your work output in joules, you need to multiply the watts by the number of seconds over which the power has been applied.

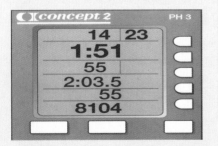

TEAM RACING

It is now possible for crews of four or eight to compete on rowing machines, and for the audience to see on a large screen the two virtual boats racing each other. It is even possible to compete with another individual or crew over the Internet.

MOVING ON TO THE WATER

As well as developing as a new sport in its own right, indoor rowing is a great way to teach the action of rowing and for training when it is not convenient or possible to get out on the water. Most rowing clubs now have 'ergos' and use them to measure progress in fitness development, and to provide beginners with a 'feel' for the correct rowing action before their first outing in a boat.

THE BIGGEST RACE

The British Indoor Rowing Championship (BIRC) takes place in the National Indoor Arena in Birmingham annually.

• With over 3,000 entrants, the event is the world's biggest indoor rowing race.
• It is also the biggest mass-participation indoor sporting event in Britain to date.

Competitors range from 11 to 90+ years old, including many members of the Great Britain rowing squad.

 Rowers watch their own progress on a big screen.

ROWING AND HEALTH

The links between health and exercise are well established. If you take regular exercise you will be healthier and less prone to illness and injury. You are also likely to have greater self-esteem and to have more energy to cope with the challenges and opportunities that are part of everyday life in a modern society.

TAKING UP ROWING

Even a small change in the amount of exercise you take can make a big difference. Rowing is a great way to begin taking more exercise. It does not place high stress on the joints, and provides a good range of movement to improve mobility and flexibility. Rowing also exercises a large range of muscle groups. There is little skill involved in using a rowing machine, so it's possible to begin exercising within minutes of a quick introduction.

You will find rowing machines at leisure centres, fitness clubs and, of course, rowing clubs. Many rowing clubs are now teaming up with schools and community groups, to provide facilities for individuals and groups to use in a supervised, friendly environment.

▼ Rowing is a great sport to get started in, as it requires very little skill at first.

A SPORT FOR ALL

People are currently participating in rowing from the ages of 10 to 90+ and it is a sport that families can be involved in together. Many clubs will offer considerable discounts for family membership.

Even if you feel that you are unfit, overweight and lead an unhealthy lifestyle, it is not too late to begin rowing. A female member of the GB Team at the 2006 World Rowing Championships was at one time 30kg over the 61.5kg limit to row as a lightweight – and before taking up rowing she had been a binge drinker and smoker.

One of the bronze medalists in the 50–58 age range at the 2003 British Indoor Rowing Championships was a diabetic who, prior to taking up indoor rowing, had quite an unhealthy lifestyle.

Rowing can also help people improve their confidence. For example, at a height of 170cm and weighing over 76kg, Gemma Lovatt was an overweight teenager who never exercised and was being bullied at school. 'Trust me, it's not fun,' said Gemma. 'I had no confidence, I hated my body and was allergic to any form of exercise.' Gemma decided to try rowing and on her own admission was 'scared senseless' the first time she went out in a boat.

Gemma overcame her fears and now rows regularly at a local rowing club. Talking about the rowing club, Gemma says, 'I was terrified that I wouldn't fit in, but I have made some of the best friends I've ever had. They believe in me and they never gave up on me. I even won a race in a double. I'd never won a race before in my life and felt absolutely great.' As well as health and social benefits, Gemma says her overall fitness has improved dramatically.

OVERCOMING A CHALLENGE

Sir Steve Redgrave, five times Olympic gold medalist, is a diabetic. All top athletes expend enormous amounts of energy in their training. This has to be replaced by eating lots of energy-rich foods. As a diabetic, it has been a challenge for Sir Steve to manage gaining the required energy with very limited use of sugar-based products (for most people, natural sugar is a rich source of energy). There are also other restrictions that a diabetic faces, such as eating every two hours, which can interfere with training. But, as Sir Steve has demonstrated, this can be done!

LEARNING TO ROW

The best way of learning to row is to join a club – you will find information at the back of this book on how to find the nearest club to where you live. Most clubs have a Dry Start programme, which will introduce you to the facilities, the safety code and rowing on an ergo (which shows you the most effective way of using your muscles to row).

 Young rowers practising in stable sculling boats.

ON THE WATER

Your first outing on the water is likely to be in a training boat, which is more stable than a race boat, and will allow you to build up confidence while you learn to control the boat. You will also find yourself doing confidence-building drills that might seem rather extreme – for example, standing up in the boat – but all of these steps will be carefully controlled by a coach. The aims are to make the experience fun, and to help you become a safe and confident rower.

SAFETY PROCEDURES

Part of your development as a rower will include a swim test and capsize and immersion drill. This is usually carried out at a swimming pool with a coach and lifeguard present. The aim is to teach you the safe procedures to follow in the event of a capsize when rowing. You will also need to demonstrate that you can swim 50m in light clothing.

Although racing boats are fragile and great care needs to be taken to avoid damage, training boats are made from tough materials that make them ideal for young people to learn in. They are also very stable, so that it is possible to begin rowing with very little instruction and preparation.

Practising a capsize in the safety of a swimming pool.

Balancing in a wobbly boat is rather like standing on a tightrope – you have to stay relaxed.

WHO CAN LEARN TO ROW?

Which statements would you guess are true?

To learn to row you need to be:

1) very fit and active

2) able to swim

3) good at sport

4) under 30 years of age

5) over 10 years of age

6) over 15 years of age

7) very safety conscious

8) fully able-bodied.

1) Do you need to be fit and active to start rowing?

No, people of all shapes and sizes can learn to row. It is true that to become a top rower it helps if you are tall and muscular, but many people who do not fit this profile can achieve a great deal of success in rowing. You do not have to be fit and active – if you learn to row, the chances are that you will become fitter and healthier.

2) Do you have to be a swimmer to start rowing?

Yes, you do have to be able to swim.

3) Do you have to be good at sports?

No, you do not necessarily need to be good at other sports. Many people who have failed at other sports find that they become successful rowers. If you meet a top rower, try throwing a ball for them to catch – and don't be surprised if they drop it!

4) Do you have to be under 30?

If you are reasonably active you can begin rowing at any age – and many clubs now run 'Learn to Row' courses for adults. Veteran rowing (rowing for older people) is growing enormously and it is now not

 Indoor rowing can build up your stamina and strength before you head out on to the water.

unusual to see crews with an average age of 70 competing at regattas – and many more people continue rowing for much longer. Rowing can encompass such a wide age-range because it is a low-impact sport. This means it does not concentrate stress in particular parts of the muscular-skeletal system (although see below for possible effects on juniors).

5) and 6) Are there younger age limits?

Few clubs have members below the age of nine in their juniors section, but it is possible to begin the Dry Start programme a few years earlier. Because the action of rowing with one blade can place a strain on growing bodies, boys below the age of 15 and girls below the age of 16 can only compete in sculling races.

7) and 8) Do you need to be safety conscious and able-bodied?

Rowers need to be very safety conscious, but not necessarily able-bodied, as many clubs can now offer facilities for adaptive rowing and for people with learning difficulties.

So, you have run out of excuses, unless you are unable to swim – and you could learn to swim before taking up rowing. Go for it!

▶ A younger rowing club member carries his oars to the riverbank.

GETTING FIT FOR ROWING

Becoming fit for rowing will enable you to learn the sport more easily. One of the problems many beginners face is that the muscles they are using tend to tire out quickly. Once this happens, they are unable to do things correctly. Even though they know what to do, their tired muscles do not respond in the way they want – which can be very frustrating!

Doing too much exercise too quickly will result in injury. 'Listen to your body' is good advice.

If you have any health problems, seek medical advice before increasing your level of exercise.

a little faster than you did the last time. Timing yourself means you can measure your improvement.

You can apply this technique to walking briskly, swimming or cycling. Initially, 10 minutes each day will show an improvement over seven days. Next, extend the period of time over which you exercise. Build up gradually to exercising for 30 minutes continuously.

BUILDING FITNESS FOR BEGINNERS

To improve your fitness, you need to exercise hard, then allow a period of recovery, before increasing the stress a little more the next time you train. Try walking up stairs a little faster than you normally would. Aim to feel the effect of this increased effort – but not so much that you could not repeat it almost immediately. The next time you walk up stairs, move

ROWING MUSCLES

Rowing uses more major muscle groups than any other sporting activity. The primary effects are in the legs, back and arms. As all your weight is supported by the boat there is no jarring of the joints, making rowing a very safe sport. When you become proficient you can expect to burn 500–600 calories per hour.

The main muscles used in rowing.

USING AN ERGOMETER

An ergometer enables you to exercise the muscles that are specific to rowing. Follow a pattern of gradually increasing the time and effort. You will find beginners' training programmes on the British Indoor Rowing Championships website (www.concept2.co.uk/birc/).

As you begin rowing, your fitness will improve in two main ways.

- **Aerobic fitness**
  Your heart and lungs (your cardiovascular system) will be able to work harder to deliver more oxygen to the blood. This means you can breathe harder for longer and exercise for longer periods.

- **Anaerobic fitness**
  You will be better able to produce intense effort in short bursts, such as a sprint at the end of a race.

Rowing provides a good balance between these two types of fitness and will help you develop a well-proportioned body. For example, rowers do not have the bulging muscles of weightlifters or the very lean bodies of long-distance runners.

Your induction to rowing will provide a carefully planned programme to improve your fitness – and your health in general.

> **The recovery phase of exercise is just as important as the exercise itself.**

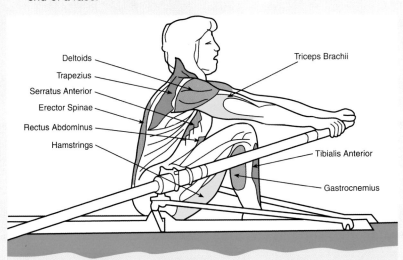

Deltoids
Trapezius
Serratus Anterior
Erector Spinae
Rectus Abdominus
Hamstrings

Triceps Brachii
Tibialis Anterior
Gastrocnemius

TAKING THE STROKE

This section introduces you to the terminology used to describe the parts of the stroke, and the body positions that will maximise the power of your muscles in moving the boat.

THE PERFECT STROKE

When you learn to row, you begin with simple exercises. The following sequence of photographs shows what you will be working towards.

THE DRIVE PHASE

This is the start of the drive phase of the stroke, when the blades are placed in the water (called 'the catch') and the boat is driven forwards using the large muscle groups in the legs and body.

- The shins are vertical, the back straight and leaning forward and the body closed up on the thighs.

- All that is needed is for the hands to lift a little more in the direction of the arrow, and the blades will be fully 'locked' in the water.

COMMON PROBLEMS TO LOOK OUT FOR AT POINT 1

The seat begins to move backwards faster than the shoulders. This fault is known as 'bum shoving' and it causes the powerful leg drive to be weakened considerably.

It is a mistake to think that rowing is pulling with the arms, but many beginners do this.

- The legs should be doing most of the work here, with the arms relaxed and the back still straight and leaning forward.
- The hands follow the path of the arrow parallel to the boat. The feeling should be that of hanging off the blade handles.

COMMON PROBLEMS TO LOOK OUT FOR AT POINT 2

Arms pulling over into an arc causing the blades to plunge too deep.

Nearing the end of the drive phase the body swings back and the arms are used to maintain the momentum of the blade handles.

COMMON PROBLEMS TO LOOK OUT FOR AT POINT 3

The blade handle is pulled down (instead of along) causing the blade to lift from the water before the end of the stroke. This is called 'washing out'.

The hands make a small tap downwards, to lift the blades clear of the water.

- The legs are flat down.
- The back is straight, but leaning slightly back so that the abdominal muscles feel a slight pull.
- The blade handles just brush the body when the spoon end is flat on the water.

This is the end of the drive phase and the recovery phase begins.

COMMON PROBLEMS TO LOOK OUT FOR AT POINT 4

The rower sits too upright and the elbows droop down – the effect is to shorten the stroke.
The rower leans too far back – which delays the recovery.

THE RECOVERY PHASE

At the beginning of the recovery phase, the hands move down and away, following the trajectory of the arrow.

- The arms move away from the body, which is balanced vertically, but the seat has not yet begun to move and the knees are still held down.
- The arms, shoulders and neck are relaxed. This posture aids recovery from the exertion of the stroke, and helps to keep the boat balanced in the water.
- The body then rocks over from the pelvis, with the back straight, and the knees lift, allowing the seat to move.

COMMON PROBLEMS TO LOOK OUT FOR AT POINT 5

The knees lift and get in the way of the hands, which should be moving parallel to the boat.

COMMON PROBLEMS TO LOOK OUT FOR AT POINT 6

The hands are higher or lower than the point shown. The body is not leaning forward at the angle shown. The rower does not slow forward momentum before taking the catch.

COMMON PROBLEMS TO LOOK OUT FOR AT POINT 8

The rower does not reach forward to get a long stroke. The body collapses over the knees. The shins are not vertical.

COMMON PROBLEMS TO LOOK OUT FOR AT POINT 7

The body is upright and the arms are not held out long enough.

The body at this point is in the catch position, moving forward until the shins are vertical and the sequence begins again.

together for the first time the boat tends to flop from side to side, which makes it very difficult to row properly.

Sitting the boat (keeping it level)

In a boat full of beginners, at least two people will often not be rowing at all, but sitting still with their blades touching the water. They are working in a similar way to stabilisers on a toddler's bike, keeping the boat stable in the water. This is called 'sitting the boat'. More experienced crews will be able to balance the boat perfectly when the blades are out of the water.

You will also see experienced rowers practising their rowing action with two people sitting the boat.

WHAT TO LOOK FOR

Beginner rowers in particular can learn a great deal by watching and listening. Here are some of the things they should aim to see and hear.

Watching beginners in action

You will notice that beginners in a crew often have difficulty getting the blades in and out of the water in time with the others in the boat (called 'getting the timing right'). Learning to move and act in perfect unison in a crew is one of the challenges in learning to row.

You might have noticed that racing boats are hardly wider than a canoe and therefore when the blades are out of the water in the recovery phase, it is like balancing on a tightrope. When beginners row

PART OF A CREW

It can sometimes be very frustrating when you are learning to row in a crew. Rowing in a single is one thing, but when you row in a crew, everyone has do the same thing at the same time. However, once you achieve this, the feeling of speed and togetherness that comes from rowing together as a crew is a great sensation.

CLOTHING

Whatever the weather, the clothes will be close-fitting, to avoid loose clothing jamming any of the mechanisms in the boat. The clothing will also be made up of relatively thin layers, the colder the weather, the more layers. Multiple layers are more easily removed or put on as the conditions change. The key is to avoid getting too hot (hyperthermia) or too cold (hypothermia). You will also notice that each member of the crew has a drinks bottle with them. If they are exercising hard, they need to avoid becoming dehydrated.

On your first outing in a boat, wear layers of close-fitting clothing and bring a drinks bottle with you. Baggy shorts with floppy T-shirts hanging out are not suitable.

This rowing boat has been adapted for use by rowers with disabilities.

LISTENING TO A COX

A wired-for-sound cox gives instructions to her crew.

Getting the boat on to the water
When the cox takes command of a crew to get the boat out of the boathouse and on to the water, you will hear a series of commands. These will get the crew to:

- lift the boat up carefully
- move the boat out of the boathouse
- get the boat on to the water.

The crew works in complete unison, otherwise they might drop the boat or cause damage if it catches on obstacles.

'Number off from bow when ready'
With the boat in the water and the blades in position, the cox will command the crew into the boat. Before setting off he/she will check that everyone is ready by calling 'Number off from bow when ready'.

Starting the boat
To get the crew rowing the cox will give the sequence of commands 'Backstops… Ready… Row!' The backstops position is at the end of the drive phase, so to begin rowing, most crews start with the recovery phase.

Stopping the boat

To get the crew to stop rowing, the cox warns them that a command is about to be given by calling 'Next stroke'. At the beginning of the next stroke the cox will give the command 'Easy oars'.

With beginners, a cox will often call commands in time with the stroke, so that the N of 'next' and E of 'easy' will be in time with the catch, and the K of 'stroke' and S of 'oars' are stressed at the point at which the blades are extracted from the water, called the 'finish'.

There are variations in the terminology and procedures used, but you should be able to work out what is happening in response to the cox's commands.

Cox's position in the boat

In some fours, the cox is at the front of the boat almost lying down, so that only his or her head is visible. This kind of boat is known as a bow loader. In bow loaders, the cox steers with a small lever.

In other fours and in all eights, the cox is at the stern of the boat and steers with handles in each hand, which are connected to the rudder.

Watch very carefully and you will see that a good cox only steers when the blades are in the water taking a stroke. This is because steering when the blades are out of the water upsets the balance of the boat.

COXLESS BOATS

Not all boats have a cox. In a coxless boat the person doing the steering usually gives the commands.

I'M A COX – GET ME IN THE BOAT!

China is planning a television reality show to select two coxes for the Beijing Olympics. The entire Chinese population of 1.3 billion people will have a chance to vote in the selection process.

A cox giving the crew encouragement.

LISTENING TO A COACH

Try to listen to a coach talking (or shouting) to a crew. You are very likely to hear the following comments.

'Control the slide, slow down as you approach the catch'
Crashing forward and stopping suddenly to take the catch stops the momentum of the boat, and can result in poor control of the blade.

'Square early'
In the recovery phase, the blade is flat (called the feathered position). This is important to reduce wind resistance, but if the blade is feathered too late it might not be vertical (in the square position) in time to make a powerful stroke. So the coach wants the crew to move the blade to the square position a little earlier than they are doing.

'You're early, Two'
This is to indicate to the person in the Two Seat that their stroke is not in time with the rest of the crew – in this case too early.

'Three, you're bum shoving'
The person in the Three Seat is being warned that their seat (and therefore their bum) is moving ahead of their shoulders at the beginning of the stroke.

'Let the boat run'
In the recovery phase of the stroke it's important to stay relaxed and balanced, and to slow down before taking the next stroke. This allows the boat to run, or glide, further between strokes, and is vital for moving the boat effectively.

A loudspeaker and bicycle: two essential tools of the rowing coach's trade.

'I want to see bigger puddles'

The puddles are the swirls of water that the blades make when they leave the water. The bigger the puddle, the greater (and more effective) the effort. So the coach is telling the crew to work harder!

'Feel for the balance'

The coach has noticed that the boat is not perfectly balanced, and wants the crew to correct this. They need to feel connected to the boat through their feet, and to make tiny shifts of weight low down in their hips.

'Hands, body, slide'

Here the coach is reminding the crew that the sequence at the beginning of the recovery phase is hands moving away first, then the body rocks over, then the seat begins to move on the slide.

Part of the role of the cox is to remind the crew of important coaching points, so you might well hear him/her shouting similar comments.

If you do not understand what a coach is asking you to do, ask for clarification.

A coach cycles along the towpath to keep up with the boat.

Coaches often write down training times on a clipboard, to measure the crew's progress.

35

PRACTICE DRILLS

As a new rower you will find yourself doing lots of practice drills. Drills can help you progress in all areas of rowing, whether it be coordination, blade control, acceleration and/or balance.

COMMON DRILLS

Here are three of the drills rowers do.

1. Arms only, that is, sitting at the backstops position and using only the arms to row with.

2. Arms and body only rowing, that is rocking the body over to lengthen the stroke.

3. Using only the first quarter of the slide – which is called quarter-slide rowing. Similarly, half-slide and three-quarter-slide rowing.

These exercises break up the stroke into different parts to improve the technique for each part, and they are frequently used as warm-up exercises.

> Practice drills will help improve your rowing and enable you to make faster progress.

OTHER PRACTICE DRILLS

1. With square blades; i.e. not feathering

Rowing with square blades enables you to concentrate on the feeling of placing the blade in the water at the correct point (the catch) and of extracting it square rather than feathering the blade when it is still partially in the water.

2. With one hand off the blade (but only in rowing, not sculling!)

Rowing with the outside hand (the hand nearest the end of the blade handle) takes more of the load at the catch and does most of the tap down at the end of the drive phase. The inside hand does the squaring and feathering.

3. The first part of the stroke, up to the point of placing the blade in the water (a drill called roll ups)

This is to practise slowing and controlling the slide at the end of the recovery phase, and to place the blade with a relaxed and slight upwards movement of the hands.

4. Pausing at different points in the stroke during the recovery phase

This is to check body positions, and to feel for the balance, using pressure on the toes and slight shifts of weight low down in the hips to connect you to the boat.

Cambridge stroke Kristopher McDaniel (right) and cox Peter Rudge during a practice session on the River Thames.

USING DRILLS

Practice drills are not just for beginners. You will see the top rowers in the world going through similar routines to maintain and improve their technique.

Oxford's Barney Williams during a practice session on the River Thames ahead of the Boat Race.

HYDRATION, NUTRITION AND HYGIENE

Hydration, hygiene and nutrition are crucial aspects of any athlete's approach to sport. They can make a huge difference to performance, whether at a club training session or an international competition.

HYDRATION

Your skin is the main regulator of your body temperature. When you get too hot exercising, your skin opens up sweat glands to produce a thin layer of moisture on its surface. This moisture is evaporated by heat energy from your body, effectively cooling you down.

Your cooling system – the amount of water in your body – needs to be topped up regularly, to replace the fluid (sweat) lost from the surface of the skin. Even if you are not sweating much, you will be losing moisture from your mouth as you breathe more quickly. If you do not replace this fluid by drinking regularly when you exercise, you risk becoming dehydrated and overheating.

NUTRITION

Food is fuel for the body, so planning a healthy diet to keep your body's tank topped up is important. Athletes also need to plan for recovery snacks immediately after exercising. After strenuous exercise

EFFECTS OF FLUID LOSS

You can keep a check how much fluid you have lost by weighing yourself before and after exercise.

Bodyweight lost in sweat	Effect
2%	Impaired performance
4%	Reduced muscle capacity
5%	Heat exhaustion
7%	Hallucination
10%	Heat stroke – possibly fatal

your immune system can become depressed, so you are more at risk from infection. A carbohydrate snack taken within 10 minutes of completing exercise gives your immune system a quick boost.

As a guide, for a recovery snack you need the following (per 1.5kg of your bodyweight):

After light training

- 0.5g of carbohydrate
- 0.05–0.1g of protein

After heavy training

- 1.0g of carbohydrate
- 0.1–0.2g of protein

For example if you weigh 60kg you will require after a light training session:

- 60/1.5 x 0.5g of carbohydrate = 20g
- 60/1.5 x 0.05g of protein = 2g

You will find these amounts of carbohydrate and protein in snack bars and also in fruit drinks. Check what is stated on the label!

A recovery snack should be an additional part of your diet and not replace a main meal.

PLANNED INTAKE

Make your nutritional and fluid intake part of your overall training plan. With careful planning, what you eat and drink will make you feel good and help you perform to your full potential.

HYGIENE

Before you eat your recovery snack, wash your hands! The recovery snack boosts your immune system – don't expose yourself while eating it to infections on your hands. It is also important to shower after exercise and to keep your kit clean and fresh.

Making sure you drink enough water is crucial for rowing, as for all exercise.

ROLES AND RESPONSIBILITIES

Safety is of great importance in a sport that takes place on open water, where the conditions can quickly turn dangerous. It is important to understand the part that you and others play in keeping rowing a safe sport.

RESPONSIBILITIES OF A BEGINNER

If you are under 18 then your parent/s or care giver/s are responsible for you, and will be involved in checking that you are taking responsibility for:

- disclosing any relevant health problems (for example a problem with asthma). Most clubs will then be able to make provision to allow you to take part safely

- being able to swim the minimum distance set by the club. This might vary depending on the local conditions

- wearing clothing that is appropriate to the conditions. You will be given advice on this but come prepared with lots of layers

- accepting the advice and direction of the coaches.

If you are over 18 then you are responsible for yourself!

A personal flotation device (PFD) helps keep you afloat after an accident.

After your induction course with the club, you will be responsible for:

- checking the safety of the equipment that you are using (for example checking that the boat has a bow ball and that all watertight hatches are closed)

- wearing a personal flotation device (PFD), understanding and having practised its operation, until given permission not to, and when coxing a boat

- knowing what to do if the boat you are in capsizes or begins to sink

- knowing how to use emergency equipment such as a throw line to reach someone in the water

- knowing about the local hazards and navigation rules

- safe procedures for getting in and out of the boat

- safe procedures for lifting and carrying boats and equipment

- returning boats and equipment safely, and reporting any damage or problems

- knowing what not to wear – for example wellington boots that are dangerous in the event of a capsize

- keeping a log of your own progress and development.

This appears to be a formidable list, but it is part of ensuring a safe system for you and those you row with.

CAPSIZE

In the event of a capsize, remember the key points in your training.

- Stay with the boat – do NOT swim away from it.
- Swim with the boat to the nearest bank.

Wind, current flow, tides and bridges can make rowing hazardous. If in doubt, DON'T GO OUT!

 Throwing a line to someone in the water could save their life.

THE ROLES AND RESPONSIBILITIES OF THE COX

Imagine being the captain of a river boat that is 18m long and 6m wide, with a top speed of 10 knots. If you are coxing an eight, that is effectively the size and speed of the boat you are in command of.

These two boats cover the same area, but the eight will be considerably faster.

The cox plays a critical role in establishing and maintaining a safe system. In particular the cox needs to gain the respect of the crew by being confident, giving clear commands and providing useful feedback, so that the crew respond quickly and positively.

The cox is in command from the point at which the crew are ready to lift and carry the boat out of the boathouse until the point that the boat is washed down, the blades racked and the boat returned to its storage rack. The cox's responsibilities include:

Awareness of local conditions

- Knowing the local navigation rules.

- Knowing the local hazards, such as weirs and bridges, and the speed of the current or tide.

- In discussion with the coach, making a risk assessment of the weather and water conditions in relation to the experience of the crew.

Checks before boating

- Inspecting the hull for damage, checking the bow ball is in place, checking heel restraints and watertight hatches.

- Checking that the crew is dressed appropriately for the conditions.

- Liaising with the coach over the plan for the training session.

- Checking own clothing and personal flotation device (PFD).

The bow ball helps to prevent damage caused by the sharp-pointed bow of the boat in the event of a collision.

BECOMING A COX

A cox makes a great contribution to the way in which a crew perform. If this is a role that interests you then contact your local club. Most clubs are short of coxes and offer free membership and training.

During the outing

- Controlling and steering the boat by giving clear commands to the crew.

- Awareness of and respect for other water users such as fishermen and power boat users.

- Providing feedback and encouragement to the crew on basic coaching points.

- Responding to changes in conditions: i.e. returning early if conditions are worsening.

After the outing

- Checking the boat for damage and reporting any problems.

- Helping with crew debrief: i.e. providing feedback on good points and areas for improvement.

- Reflecting on how their own performance could have been improved.

The heel restraints prevent the shoes from lifting so that the feet slip out of the shoes.

THE ROLE OF THE PERSON IN THE STROKE SEAT

 A coach shouts encouragement from the riverbank.

In any boat with two or more people, the person nearest to the stern is called the 'stroke'. It is the stroke's role to set the rate and the rhythm of the rowing strokes. It is the role of the rest of the crew to follow.

THE ROLES AND RESPONSIBILITIES OF THE COACH

Rowing as a sport is not something that you can start doing on your own. It is highly technical, uses expensive equipment and takes place in an environment that is potentially dangerous. Therefore, when people learn to row they need to be taught by a coach.

Most coaches are volunteers and gain their rewards from seeing the people they coach make progress and develop as rowers. Progress is not necessarily winning races; it can also be about achieving personal goals, such as improving fitness, being able to row independently in a sculling boat, or being part of a group that rows together for social reasons. Your coach will help you to set and achieve your own goals.

A coach's responsibilities can include:

- induction courses and safety briefings for new members, both beginners and experienced rowers

- being involved in safety audits of the club's facilities and equipment

- planning training programmes for different groups
- keeping up-to-date with best practice
- being responsible for their own continuing professional development (CPD) as a coach.

A coach must have a thorough knowledge of:

- the local hazards and navigation rules
- where the first-aid kit is kept
- what the emergency procedures are in the event of an accident
- how to use the rescue aids available
- the means of checking if rowers have completed the swim test and capsize and immersion drill
- good practice in terms of child protection policies.

Before an outing a coach must:

- make a risk assessment of the conditions in relation to the experience of the rowers
- check that adequate safety checks have been made on the boats and equipment to be used
- check for inadequate clothing or signs of ill health
- agree and set realistic training goals
- liaise with the cox (if using coxed boats) on the plan for the session

- be prepared to be flexible in respect of the conditions or responses of the rowers
- speak with the rowers at the end of training, highlighting good points and areas for improvement.

Gone are the times when coaches shouted only negative comments at rowers. Modern coaching philosophy is participant-focused, with the emphasis on praise, encouragement and enthusiasm. Most coaches now have a thorough understanding of the different ways in which people learn, and can adapt their approach accordingly. Coaching is a process based on listening to participants, providing feedback and helping them to understand how they learn best.

BECOMING A COACH

It is not necessary to have been a rower to become a coach, although it does help to know the basic terminology and mechanics of the stroke. If you are interested in coaching, make contact with your local club and arrange to shadow a coach, and then perhaps investigate the coaching courses offered by the Amateur Rowing Association (details on page 52).

COMPETITIONS

For many rowers, winning competitions is their main aim. The regatta season lasts from May to September, with local club regattas being held around the country on most weekends.

 Pulling away from the start of a six-lane race.

NOVICE CLASS

When you begin rowing you are a 'novice'. You lose this title when you win a novice race at an ARA-affiliated competition that includes at least three other crews entered. Novice races are almost exclusively in coxed fours (4+) or eights (8+).

SENIOR CLASS

When you win your first qualifying race you will lose novice status and become a 'senior' rower from which you can, by winning events at each level, progress to 'elite' status.

Because rowing and sculling have separate divisions, it is possible for someone to be an elite rower yet remain a novice sculler. Novice sculling races are almost exclusively in single sculling boats (1x).

RACE FORMAT

Most of the racing takes place with crews racing side by side in two lanes, over 500–2,000m. Some larger regattas have six-lane courses. The losing crew is knocked out of the competition and the winning crew progresses to the next round. In multi-lane racing, losing crews sometimes have a second chance through a repêchage system which allows the fastest losers to reach the final.

OTHER CLASSES

There are divisions for juniors from age 9 to 18. The age division is determined by being under the specified age by the 1st September preceding the event.

There are also divisions for veteran rowers and for adaptive rowers. You might be surprised to find that if you are aged 30 then you can race as a veteran. It is the average age of a crew that counts and there are divisions with approximately five-year steps between them.

Adaptive rowing currently includes divisions for rowing with the arms only, the trunk and arms only, and other disabilities, including hearing and sight impairment and learning difficulties. The boats are specially adapted to be suitable and safe for these athletes (see pages 50–51).

HEAD OF THE RIVER

From September to April is the Head of the River race season. These 'head races' are in the form of time trials, with crews following each other at two- or three-minute intervals. These races do not qualify rowers to move between divisions: for example, a novice crew can win lots of head races without losing novice status at a regatta.

In order to race you must become a member of the ARA. Membership includes a licence to race.

 Adaptive-class rowers use specially adapted boats.

47

TAKING PART IN A RACE

Imagine that you are going to take part in your first race. You will have spent several weeks training for this event so that your coach feels that you are fully prepared.

RACING AWAY FROM HOME

For a regatta away from your own club, you will have spent time removing the riggers from the boat (called de-rigging) and loading it on to a trailer. Putting the boat back together on arrival is called rigging. One of the crew takes the crew's ARA cards to Registration, and you get a crew number, which is displayed on the backs of the cox and bow.

 Rowing boats gathered prior to a race.

GETTING TO THE START

Your coach will talk you through the race plan.

- Be on the water in time to be at the start area with at least 10 minutes to spare.

- Allow time for an umpire to check that your boat is safe to use.

You need to be familiar with the navigation up to the start area. As you are moving up, other crews will be racing down and you need to keep well clear of them. This is mainly the cox's responsibility but you need to know what to expect.

As you move up to the start area, umpires will give you instructions and the cox must act on these promptly.

THE START

The start might be a free start with the boats being lined up by the starter, or the stern of your boat might be held by someone in a boat anchored in the river. These are called stake boats. When the boats are correctly aligned, the starter will call out the names of both clubs, then call 'Attention ... Go!'

The first 10 strokes are likely to be quick and short. The aim is to get the boat moving quickly and to nose ahead of the other crew. Next, the cox will call for a lower rate and a longer stroke, which you can maintain over the whole course. The other crew can be so close that you think the blades might clash – but you must concentrate on what is happening with your own crew.

THE FINISH

As the finish line approaches, the cox calls for an extra effort and the crew respond well. You just manage to get the bows of your boat in front as you approach the line. You've won!

After a few minutes recovery, the losing crew give you three cheers and you respond in the same way.

UMPIRES

The role of the umpires and race officials at a regatta is to ensure safety and fair play. For example, if one crew is moving out of position and could clash with their opposition, they will be given a warning. If they do not respond, they could be disqualified.

You and your crew members have to wear club kit for racing.

Watching a race from the riverbank can be a thrill, but it's even better to get involved!

ADAPTIVE ROWING

Adaptive rowing is enjoyed by people who have limited use of their lower limbs. They may be wheelchair-bound, or use prosthetic limbs. Adaptive rowing also provides opportunities for people with hearing and sight impairment, or with learning difficulties, to enjoy rowing.

Preparing for the
start of the race.

BRITISH SUCCESSES

The Great Britain Adaptive Team has won gold medals at the 2004, 2005 and 2006 Rowing World Championships, and hopes to repeat these successes in the run-up to the Paralympic Games at Beijing in 2008, where rowing will be included for the first time.

COMPETITION CATEGORIES

The present categories for World Championship competition are for:

- men and women athletes who use arms only in single boats (AM1x and AW1x)
- a crew of one man and one women using trunks and arms (TA2x)
- a crew of two men and two women in a coxed boat using legs, trunks and arms (LTA4+).

Increasingly, rowing clubs around the world are facilitating adaptive rowing by providing equipment and training coaches to support adaptive athletes.

The sport of indoor rowing also has a range of equipment and competitions for adaptive athletes.

FES ROWING

Brunel University has developed a Functional Electrical Stimulation (FES) rowing project. FES rowing uses electrical stimulation to activate the paralysed leg muscles

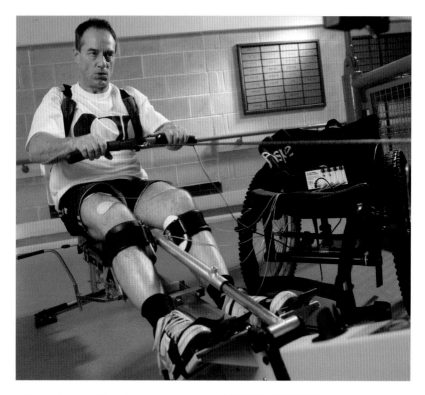

Using the FES rowing machine developed by Brunel University.

TRYING ROWING

of people with spinal-cord injury. This makes it possible for people with paralysed legs to take part in the sport of indoor rowing, and provides long-term health benefits. It is expected that up to 10 paraplegic athletes will compete alongside able-bodied competitors in the 2006 British Indoor Rowing Championship. As of 2007, the availability of this system was limited to the London area, but is it likely to become more widely available over the coming years.

If you have a physical limitation and you would like to try rowing, contact your local club and find out what they can do to support you. Alternatively they might be able to provide you with a contact for another club that does have specialist facilities and equipment. As with any sport, you will need to be clear about what you can cope with and how hard you want to push yourself – and if any existing medical conditions need to be taken into account.

RESOURCES AND INFORMATION

There is now a wide range of resources about rowing on the Internet. A few are listed below, but try using your favourite search engine to find more specific information.

For a wide range of information about membership, location of clubs, indoor rowing, coaching courses, and much more, visit the Amateur Rowing Association website at:
www.ara-rowing.org

or contact:
The ARA
6 Lower Mall
Hammersmith
London W6 9DJ
Tel: 0870 060 7100

For information about international rowing visit Fédération Internationale des Sociétés d'Aviron (FISA) at:
www.worldrowing.com/

For information about coastal rowing visit the site of the Coast Amateur Rowing Association (CARA) at:
www.rowinguk.com/index.php?sec =18
and the Cornish Pilot Gig Association at:
www.cpga.co.uk/

For information about skiff racing visit:
www.skiffing.org.uk/

For information about the British Indoor Rowing Championships, visit:
www.concept2.co.uk/birc

For information about The River and Rowing Museum at Henley, visit:
www.rrm.co.uk/

For more information about triremes, visit:
www.cma.soton.ac.uk/HistShip/ shipind.htm

Atlantic Rowing:
www.ara-rowing.org

The London Regatta Centre:
www.london-regatta-centre.org.uk

GLOSSARY

ARA Amateur Rowing Association. The national governing body for rowing in England and the UK. The ARA is responsible for Great Britain Olympic and World Rowing teams, international events in the UK, competitions and clubs, coaching, and the overall development of all types of inland, coastal and indoor rowing in England.

Back down Term used to describe using a reverse rowing action to manoeuvre the boat backwards or for turning.

Backstops The end of the slide nearest the bow. Prevents the seat from running off the slide. Also used to describe the position at which the athlete sits with their legs straight and blade to their chest.

Blade An oar.

Bow End of the boat that travels through the water first and is sharpest; athlete who sits in the seat position nearest this end of the boat.

Bow ball Ball shaped safety cap that sits over the bow end of the boat. Compulsory on all rowing boats for safety of other water users.

Bow side The right-hand (starboard) side of the boat as the cox sits or the left-hand side of the boat for a rower. Often marked by a green stripe on the oar.

Canvas The covered section of the boat that extends from the bow to the open area (where the athlete sits) and from the open area to the stern. Often used as a description of how much a race was won or lost by.

Catch The moment at which the spoon of the blade is immersed in the water and propulsive force applied. Immersion and force application should be indistinguishable actions.

Cleaver Type of blade that has a spoon in the shape of a meat cleaver.

'Come forward' Verbal instruction used by the cox or athlete to bring the crew to frontstops position ready to row.

Connection Used to describe the link between the power of an athlete's legs to the force applied to the spoon of the blade. Should be made as soon as the catch is taken and held through the trunk muscles for the length of the work section of the stroke.

Cox Person who steers the boat by means of strings or wires attached to the rudder. Can be positioned in either the stern or bow of the boat.

Coxless Boat without a cox.

Crab When the oar becomes caught in the water at the moment of extraction and the blade handle strikes the athlete. Often causes unintentional release of the blade and significant slowing of boat speed.

Double Boat for two scullers.

'Easy oar/off' Verbal instruction given by cox or athlete for crew to stop rowing.

Eight Boat for eight sweep rowers. Will always have a cox.

Ergo Indoor rowing machine.

Extraction The removal of the blade from the water by application of downward pressure to the blade handle. In sweep this is done with the outside hand on the blade handle.

Feather Blade spoon is flat to the water. This is the position of the blade spoon for the recovery section of the stroke. Athletes must be careful to fully extract the blade before feathering.

Fin A piece of metal or plastic attached to the underside of the boat towards the stern. Provides directional stability by preventing sideways slippage.

Finish The last part of the stroke where the blade handle is drawn in to the body. Following this (assuming clean extraction) the boat will be at its maximum speed. Force must be applied to the spoon right to the finish so that water does not catch up with the spoon.

FISA The Fédération Internationale des Sociétés d'Aviron is the international rowing federation. The federation is responsible for all international racing and rules. Organises a series of three World Cup Regattas and World Championships annually.

Fixed seat Either a description used to differentiate a boat without a sliding seat mechanism, or the athlete rowing arms and/or body only and therefore not moving their seat.

Four Boat for four sweep rowers. Can be coxed or coxless.

Frontstop The end of the slide nearest the stern. Prevents the seat from running off the slide. Also used to describe the position at which the athlete sits with their legs at 90°, and the blade spoon at the furthest point to the bows.

Gate The metal bar, tightened by a screw, that closes over the swivel to secure oar.

Head race Race in which crews are timed over a set distance. Usually run as a processional race rather than side by side.

Heel restraints Attached to the heels of the shoes and to the foot plate. Compulsory safety feature that helps the athlete to release their feet from the shoe in the event of a capsize.

'Hold it up' Verbal instruction meaning to bring the boat to a stop quickly. Perform an emergency stop.

Length Length of stroke – the arc through which the blade turns when it is in the water from catch to finish.

Loom The shaft of the blade from the spoon to the handle.

Macon Type of blade that has the traditional spoon shape.

Novice Term used to describe someone who has very little rowing experience.

Pair Boat for two sweep rowers.

Points Points are awarded to athletes for winning races. Number of points determines the status of the athlete. See the ARA Rules of Racing for more details.

Posture The correct body positions at different parts of the stroke cycle. See pages 26–28.

Power phase The part of the stroke between the beginning and the extraction when the blade is in the water and propelling the boat.

Pressure The amount of effort applied by the athlete to the power phase of the stroke (usually light, firm or full).

Quad Boat for four scullers.

Rate Or rating. Number of strokes rowed in a minute.

Ratio The ratio of the time taken for the power phase to that of the recovery phase of the stroke. Ideally time taken for the recovery will be about three times that of the power phase.

Recovery The part of the stroke phase between the extraction and the beginning or 'catch' when the blade is out of the water.

Regatta A competition with events for different boat types and status athletes usually involving heats, semi-finals and finals for each event. Boats compete side by side from a standing start.

Riggers Metal outriggers attached to the outer shell of the boat next to each seat, which support the swivel and the pin.

Rudder The device under the boat which, when moved, causes change of direction. Linked to the cox or a crew member by wires.

Running start A racing start undertaken with the boat already moving.

Saxboard The sides of the boat above the waterline, made to strengthen the boat where the riggers attach.

Scull Smaller version of the oar used for sculling.

Sculling Rowing with two oars.

Slide Two metal runners on which the seat travels.

Spoon The end of the oar which enters the water. Usually painted in the colours of the club represented by the athlete.

Square or squaring To turn the oar so that the spoon is at 90° to the water. This action should be done early during the recovery to ensure good preparation for the catch.

Stakeboat An anchored boat or pontoon from which rowing boats are held prior to a race starting.

Standing start A racing start done from stationary.

Stern The end of the boat that travels through the water last.

ROWING CHRONOLOGY

800 BC The first recorded history of oars being used to propel boats.

AD 1716 Doggett's Coat and Badge race is established.

1700s Rowing is introduced at Oxford University in the late 1700s.

1806 Rowing arrived at Eton College.

1812 *The Newquay*, one of the earliest Cornish Pilot gigs, is built.

1814 The oldest regatta in the rowing calendar, Chester, founded.

1815 The first eight-man boats appeared at Brasenose College, Oxford.

1815 Leander, the oldest club still in existence, is founded.

1828 Anthony Brown of Newcastle-upon-Tyne developed the outrigger for racing boats.

1829 The first Oxford v Cambridge Boat Race is staged at Henley.

1830 Wingfield Sculls for amateur champions of the Thames is founded.

1833 First record of women racing rowing boats for money.

1834 Foundation of Durham Regatta.

1839 Henley Regatta is established.

1842 The first publication on rowing as a sport: *A Treatise on the Art of Rowing as practised at Cambridge*.

1843 Oxford defeat Cambridge with only seven oarsmen (one was ill).

1855 The first keelless boats built by Matt Taylor are used by the Royal Chester Club to win at Henley.

1861 First publication of *The British Rowing Almanack*.

1863 Robert Chambers for Tyneside wins the first World Championship sculling contest.

1872 Britain's first international competition came to Henley.

1875 Invention of the swivel oarlock by Michael Davis, an American.

1882 Amateur Rowing Association is formed.

1890 National Rowing Association is formed.

1892 The Fédération Internationale des Sociétés d'Aviron (FISA) is founded.

1896 Furnival sculling club for women is formed by FJ Furnival because of his belief that 'the exclusion of women from aquatic sport is pernicious'.

1896 First crossing of the Atlantic by rowing boat. Two American fishermen, Harbo and Samuelson, rowed from New York to Ireland.

1900 First Olympic Regatta is staged in Paris.

1908 The Olympic Regatta is held at Henley. British crews win four gold medals.

1923 Women's Amateur Rowing Association is formed.

1926 Steve Fairbairn establishes the Thames Head of the River Race.

1947 British crews compete at the European Championships for the first time.

1956 National and Amateur Rowing Associations merge.

1963 Women's ARA merges with ARA.

1967 First FISA Junior Regatta.

1969 First solo crossing of the Atlantic by rowing boat. Tom McClean rows from Newfoundland to Ireland.

1973 Britain opens its first multi-lane international course in Nottingham.

1975 World Championships are staged at Nottingham.

1976 Women's rowing is first included in the Olympic Games.

1986 World Championships are staged at Nottingham.

2004 Steve Redgrave wins his fifth consecutive Olympic gold medal.

2005 Rowing World Cup is held at Dorney Lake, Eton.

2006 Rowing World Championships are held at Dorney Lake, Eton.

2012 Olympic rowing events are to be held at Dorney Lake, Eton.

SOME SUCCESSFUL BRITISH ROWERS

Zac Purchase

Zac is one of Britain's most talented young scullers, having won the World U23 title in a single scull in 2005 before carrying on to the World Championships later that year to take a world silver medal in this event. He became World Champion in 2006 in this class, winning gold on home water at Eton in a world's best time.

Helene Rainsford

Helene became World Champion in the arms only single (AW1x) in her first international rowing competition, leading from the start to win by 8 seconds over USA and Poland. She is the current British record holder in women's arms only single scull for 1km on the water and British Indoor Rowing fixed seat 2km ergometer champion.

Previously, Helene competed as part of the Great Britain Women's Wheelchair Basketball Team who won Paralympic World Cup silver medals in 2005 and 2006. Helene is a medical biochemist and is currently project manager for a sexual health screening programme in Surrey.

Steve Williams MBE

Steve became Olympic Champion in Athens in 2004 when the men's four crossed the line first in one of the most exciting finishes ever seen. He then went on to take gold in both the 2005 and 2006 World Rowing Championships, taking his personal tally to four World titles. Steve also won World Championship gold in the pair in 2000 and in the four in 2001.

▼ From right: Great Britain's Andrew Triggs Hodge, Alex Partridge, Peter Reed and Steve Williams celebrate their win in the men's four final, 2006.

Katherine Granger MBE

Katherine is Britain's most successful Olympic female rower, winning silver medals at the Athens and Sydney Olympics. She was a member of the quadruple scull that won gold at the World Championships in 2005 and in 2006. Katherine is a very versatile rower, having won medals in both rowing and sculling. Katherine has completed bachelors and masters degrees in law and is now studying for a PhD.

Sir Matthew Pinsent CBE

One of our best known sportsmen, Matthew Pinsent's rowing career spanned 17 years, during which time he has won 10 World Championship gold medals and four Olympic gold medals.

Whilst studying geography at Oxford University Matthew also won two Oxford v Cambridge Boat Races. He is now working as a sports journalist and is a regular television presenter with BBC News 24.

Sir Steve Redgrave CBE

Steve Redgrave is one of the greatest Olympic athletes ever, being the first athlete to win five gold medals at consecutive Olympic Games in an endurance event. He has also won 10 World Championship gold medals and is also a former World Champion indoor rower. As well as being one of the best rowers in the world, Steve is a former member of the Great Britain bobsleigh team.

In 1997 Steve was diagnosed with diabetes. He not only learned to manage this condition, but went on to win two more World Championship medals and one more Olympic gold medal.

Steve is currently involved in developing rowing as a sport for young people and in promoting health and sports medicine.

From right: Rebecca Romero, Sarah Winckless, Frances Houghton and Katherine Grainger of Great Britain celebrate after winning the gold medal in the women's quadruple sculls final at the 2005 World Rowing Championships.

INDEX